Christmas Carols

Arranged by Marjorie Wyckoff
Illustrated by Corinne Malvern

A GOLDEN BOOK · NEW YORK

O Jesu Sweet, O Jesu Mild

Scheidt's Tablaturbuch, 1650
"O Jesulein suss, O Jesulein mild"

Harmonization (simplified) by J. S. Bach

O   Je - su   sweet,   O   Je - su

mild, O love - ly Babe, Ce - les - tial Child! Thou cam'st to us from Heav'n a - bove To bring poor mor - tals God's great love O Je - su sweet, O Je - su mild!

O Jesu sweet, O Jesu mild,
Help us to do Thy holy will.
Lo, all our lives are Thine alone,
Since, in our hearts,
    Thy love has shone.
O Jesu sweet, O Jesu mild.

Away in a Manger

Martin Luther

German Folk Song

A - way in a man - ger, no crib for a bed, The

lit - tle Lord Je - sus laid down His sweet head; The

stars in the sky___ Looked down where He lay, The

lit - tle Lord Je - sus, A - sleep in the hay.

Joy to the World

From Psalm 92
Isaac Watts, 1719

George Frideric Handel, 1742

Joy to the world! The Lord is come; Let earth re-ceive her

King; Let ev-'ry heart pre-pare Him room, And

heav'n and na-ture sing, And heav'n and na-ture

And heav'n and na-ture sing, And

sing, And heav'n, and heav'n and na-ture sing.

heav'n and na-ture sing, And heav'n and na-ture sing.

See the blazing Yule before us,

Fa, la, la, la, la, la, la, la, la.

Strike the harp and join the chorus,

Fa, la, la, la, la, la, la, la, la.

Follow me in merry measure,

Fa, la, la, la, la, la, la, la, la.

While I tell of Yuletide treasure,

Fa, la, la, la, la, la, la, la, la.

The First Nowell

Words Traditional

Traditional English Melody

The first Now - ell the an - gel did say Was to
cer - tain poor shep-herds in fields as they lay; In fields where
they lay keep-ing their sheep, On a cold win-ter's night that
was_ so deep. Now - ell,_ Now - ell, Now - ell, Now-
ell._ Born is the King_ of Is - ra - el.

While Shepherds Watched Their Flocks

Rev. Nathan Tate, 1696

George Frideric Handel

O Come, All Ye Faithful

Anonymous Latin Hymn, 17th or 18th Century
Translated by Fred. Oakley, 1841

J. F. Wades Cantus Diversi, *1751*

O come, all ye faith-ful, joy-ful and tri-umph-ant, O come ye, O come ye to Beth - le -hem;

O Christmas Tree

Ernst Anschütz, after a 16th-Century Folk Song

Traditional German Tune

O Christ - mas tree, O Christ - mas tree, Your branches green de - light us. They're green when sum - mer days are bright; They're green when win - ter snow is white. O Christ - mas tree, O Christ - mas tree, Your branches green de - light us!

He Is Sleeping

George Wolfson

Polish Carol, 16th Century
Arranged by Marjorie Wyckoff

Chil - dren, come and see Him slum - ber, In the

man - ger soft with hay. He, our bless - ed lit - tle

Sav - iour, There was born to us to - day. O ye watch-ers, play sweet mu - sic, Sing you now your songs of cheer,

softly

For our Sav-iour now is here, For our Sav-iour now is here.

I Saw Three Ships

Traditional English   *Traditional Air from Derbyshire*

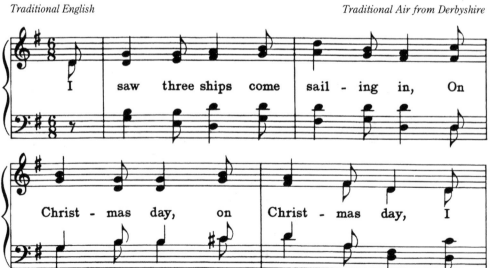

I saw three ships come sail - ing in, On Christ - mas day, on Christ - mas day, I

saw three ships come sail - ing in, On

Christ - mas day in the morn - ing!

Silent Night

Joseph Mohr, 1816
Translator Anonymous

Franz Grüber

Hark! the Herald Angels Sing

Charles Wesley

Felix Mendelssohn

Hark! the her-ald an-gels sing, "Glo-ry to the new-born King!

Peace on earth and mer-cy mild, God and sin-ners re-con-ciled?"

Joy-ful, all ye na-tions rise, Join the tri-umph of the skies;

With th'an-gel-ic host pro-claim, "Christ is born in Beth-le-hem!"

Hark! the her-ald an-gels sing, "Glo-ry to the new-born King!"